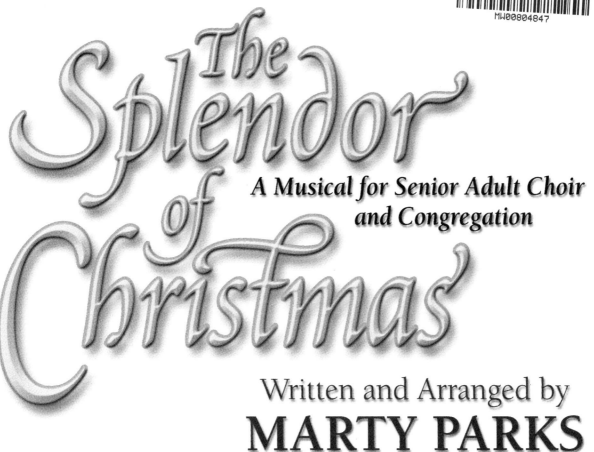

The Splendor of Christmas

A Musical for Senior Adult Choir and Congregation

Written and Arranged by
MARTY PARKS

Contents

LILLENAS
PUBLISHING COMPANY

lillenas.com

The Splendor of Christmas

Words and Music by
MARTY PARKS
Arranged by Marty Parks

Bright and festive ♩ = ca. 104

The won - der of a Prom - ise from

fills   the earth   with   joy   Is   God   Him -

self   ap - pear - ing   as   a   ba - by   boy!_____   The

won - der of   a   Prom - ise   from   Heav - en,

9

NARRATOR *(without music)*: Ah, yes, Christmas! I know it's hard to believe, but an entire year has passed since we last shared in the wonder, the joy, the…well, the splendor of Christmas. Lots has happened, hasn't it? Some of it was good and some of it was frightening. Our world changes daily and is in desperate need of a good word.

"How beautiful on the mountains are the feet of those who bring good news, who proclaim…peace." *(Isaiah 52:7)* Those are the words of the prophet Isaiah from many centuries ago. Looking around today, we may have difficulty finding any semblance of true, lasting peace. *(music begins)* But listen closely– God is still whispering, "Peace on earth, good will to men."

I Heard the Bells of Christmas Day

with
Prince of Peace

HENRY WADSWORTH LONGFELLOW

JEAN BAPTISTE CALKIN
Arranged by Marty Parks

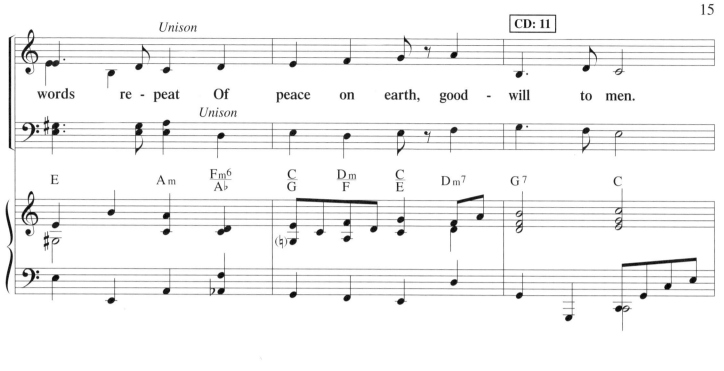

CD: 11

Unison

words re-peat Of peace on earth, good-will to men.

Unison

Solo (or Choir unison) 17 *"Prince of Peace"

Make our hearts Your throne, Prince of

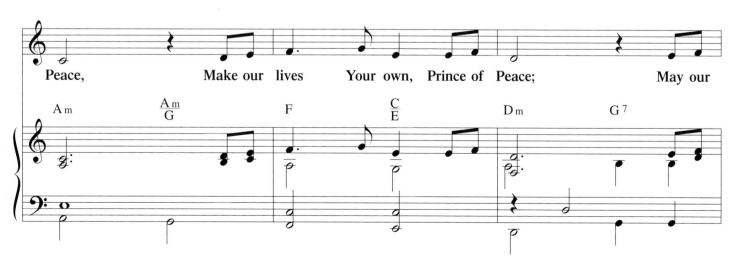

Peace, Make our lives Your own, Prince of Peace; May our

CD: 14

joy in-crease, and our striv - ing cease, As we rest in You, Prince of

Peace.

Choir and Congregation
Unison

Then pealed the bells more

Unison

loud and deep: "God is not dead, nor doth He sleep; The

Divisi

Divisi

CD: 15

NARRATOR *(without music)*: Unexpected events can shatter our sense of peace, can't they? Even when the unexpected is a word from God, the serenity of our own little world can suddenly be shaken to its core. I imagine that Mary felt this way as an angel greeted her and announced that she, of all women, had been chosen to give birth to the Messiah.

What thoughts do you think flooded her mind? What emotions swept over her soul? Mary's response is a model for us when we face the unexpected. Her acceptance of the word of the Lord resulted in an outburst of praise: "My soul magnifies the Lord!"

No doubt she remembered the words of the *(music begins)* ancient Psalmist who said, "O magnify the Lord with me, and let us exalt His name together."

Magnify the Lord

with
When Morning Gilds the Skies

Words and Music by
DAVID L. BURKUM
Arranged by Marty Parks

24

CD: 19

CD: 20

NARRATOR *(without music)*: Mary's song echoed centuries of praise and hope in the coming Messiah. Seven hundred years earlier, the prophet Isaiah had given a word picture of the majesty of this coming King. He would be wisdom, power, compassion and peace, all wrapped up in a Son. What a splendid gift He would be!

For unto Us a Child Is Born

with
The Birthday of a King

Words and Music by
JOE E. PARKS
Arranged by Marty Parks

the Prince of Peace!

CD: 24

Choir and Congregation
Unison *mf*

In the

Unison *mf*

*"The Birthday of a King"
Warmly ♩ = ca. 78

lit - tle vil - lage of Beth - le-hem, There lay a Child one

Slower

38

NARRATOR *(without music)*: And so, He came. Not as the world expected, but according to God's perfect plan. And not when the world expected, but in the fulness of God's time.

So it is today. In the busyness of the season, let's stop for just a moment and reflect on this marvelous reality. Let's put away the trappings of the season and all the noisy celebrations to simply ponder the Word made flesh, the infinite clothed in mortality, *(music begins)* Emmanuel– God with us.

We Would Worship Thee

with
Silent Night! Holy Night!

Words and Music by
JOE E. PARKS
Arranged by Marty Parks

CD: 27 Reverently ♩ = ca. 76

In this qui - et

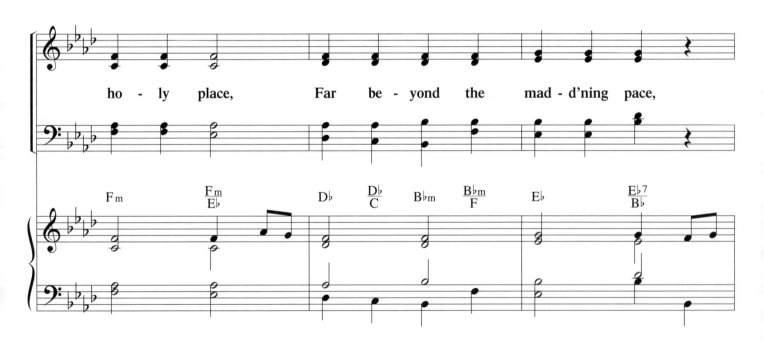

ho - ly place, Far be - yond the mad - d'ning pace,

ho - ly Child, Son of Mar - y, un - de - filed,

We would wor - ship Thee.

Trib - ute now we

43

44

Choir and Congregation
*"Silent Night! Holy Night!"

Si - lent night! ho - ly night! All is calm,

48

Joyful, Joyful, We Adore You

with
O Come, All Ye Faithful

LINDA LEE JOHNSON

LUDWIG VAN BEETHOVEN
Arranged by Marty Parks

CD: 34

Praise You for Your gift of love.

All Your works de - clare Your glo - ry; All cre - a - tion

NARRATOR *(without music)*: On the night Jesus was born, shepherds were watching their flocks in the fields outside Bethlehem. In a flash, their world was turned upside down. First an angel, then a multitude of angels, filled the skies and proclaimed the birth of the Messiah. No one had ever seen anything like that before!

Following the angels' bidding, the shepherds left for Bethlehem to find the Christ child. How excited they were! The celebration had begun!

Gloria

with
Angels, from the Realms of Glory

Words and Music by
OTIS SKILLINGS
Arranged by Marty Parks

Bright gospel ♩ = ca. 88

CD: 40

Unison Glo - ri - a, glo - ri - a!

These are the words that the an-gels sang; Choirs of heav-en-ly voic-es rang.

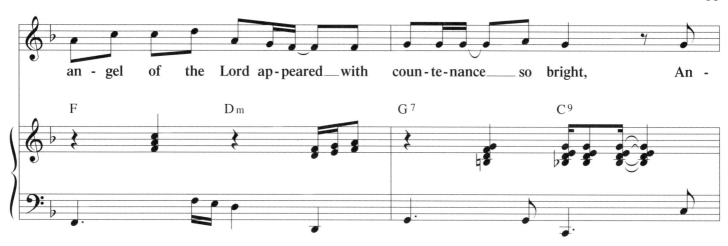

an - gel of the Lord ap-peared___with coun-te-nance___so bright, An -

nounc-ing they would find the Child___a - sleep - ing on the hay;_____ Then

CD: 43

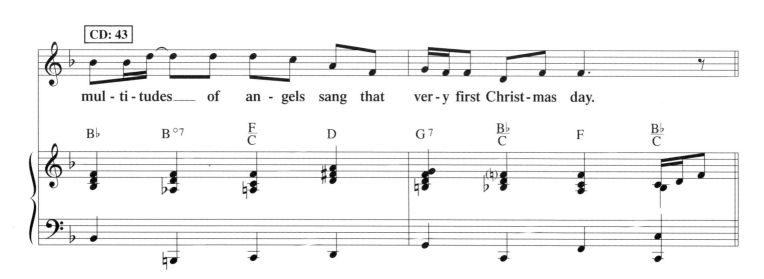

mul - ti - tudes___ of an - gels sang that ver - y first Christ - mas day.

King._____ Glory to the new-born

King.

CD: 44

accel.

accel.

Choir and Congregation ㊶ *Unison*   Faster ♩ = ca. 98   *"Angels, from the Realms of Glory"*

An - gels, from the realms of glo - ry,

Unison

NARRATOR *(without music)*: And so it happened. Not as anyone expected, but exactly as they needed. *(music begins)* In the most unusual way, and in the most out-of-the way place, Jesus– the glorious Son of God– left the splendor of heaven and all that was His, for you…for me.

I Love You, Lord Jesus

Words and Music by
MARTY PARKS
Arranged by Marty Parks

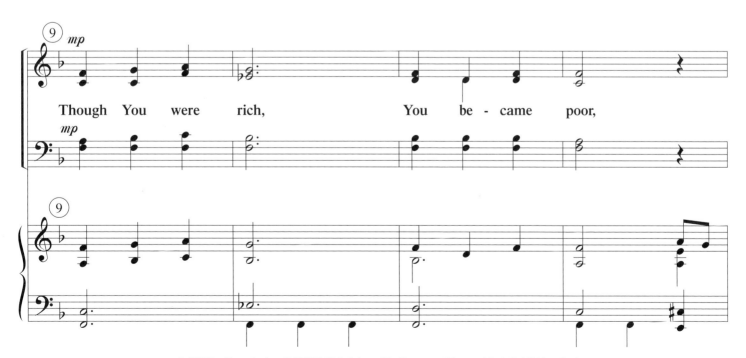

Though You were rich, You be - came poor,

PLEASE NOTE: Copying of this product is NOT covered by CCLI licenses. For CCLI information call 1-800-234-2446.

CD: 48

love You, Lord Je - sus, I love You, Lord Je - sus; You

came to this earth for me. I

love You, Lord Je - sus, I love You, Lord Je - sus; You

ри

NARRATOR *(without music)*: So you see, we don't celebrate a season. We celebrate a Savior. It's not about a single day, but about a lifetime given to Him.

Can you hear Him? Above the clamor of holiday festivities, He's speaking peace to you.

Can you see Him? Beyond the glitter and tinsel and dazzling lights, He is the true Light shining in this world's darkness.

The glory of the Father, the eternal joy of heaven; Jesus– He is the splendor of Christmas.

The Splendor of Christmas
(Reprise)

Words and Music by
MARTY PARKS
Arranged by Marty Parks

Bright and festive ♩ = ca. 104

The won - der of a Prom - ise from

CD: 53

twink - ling lights that glit - ter from a tree;

B♭M⁹   F⁶   B♭M⁹

33   CD: 54

Solo (or Men unison)
It's not a pres - ent wrapped es - pe - cial - ly for
mf

33   F⁶   B♭M⁹   F⁶   Gm⁷

37   Duet (or Choir)

me.   What makes the sea - son bright, what

F²/A   F⁶   37   B♭   B♭M⁷   C/B♭   B♭   C/B♭

Lyrics *for* Congregational Participation

I Heard the Bells on Christmas Day

I heard the bells on Christmas day
Their old familiar carols play,
And wild and sweet the words repeat
Of peace on earth, good-will to men.

And in despair I bowed my head,
"There is no peace on earth," I said,
"For hate is strong, and mocks the song
Of peace on earth, good-will to men."

Then pealed the bells more loud and deep:
"God is not dead, nor doth He sleep;
The wrong shall fail, the right prevail,
With peace on earth, good-will to men."

Words by Henry Wadsworth Longfellow
Music by Jean Baptiste Calkin

When Morning Gilds the Skies

When morning gilds the skies, My heart awaking cries:
May Jesus Christ be praised!
Alike at work and prayer, To Jesus I repair.
May Jesus Christ be praised!

Through this, His holy birth, Mankind is shown its worth;
May Jesus Christ be praised!
Adore Him, God's own Son; The precious Holy One.
May Jesus Christ be praised!

Words by *Katholisches Gesangebuch* and Marty Parks
Music by Joseph Barnby

The Birthday of a King

In the little village of Bethlehem,
There lay a Child one day,
And the sky was bright with a holy light
O'er the place where Jesus lay.

Alleluia! O how the angels sang!
Alleluia! How it rang!
And the sky was bright with a holy light;
'Twas the birthday of a King.

Alleluia! O how the angels sang!
Alleluia! How it rang!
And the sky was bright with a holy light;
'Twas the birthday of a King.

Words and Music by William Harold Neidlinger

Silent Night! Holy Night!

Silent night! holy night!
All is calm, all is bright
Round yon virgin mother and Child.
Holy infant, so tender and mild,
Sleep in heavenly peace; sleep in heavenly peace.

Silent night! holy night!
Son of God, love's pure light
Radiant beams from Thy holy face,
With the dawn of redeeming grace,
Jesus, Lord, at Thy birth, Jesus, Lord, at Thy birth.

Words by Joseph Mohr
Music by Franz Gruber

O Come, All Ye Faithful

O come, all ye faithful, joyful and triumphant.
O come ye, O come ye to Bethlehem.
Come and behold Him– born the King of angels!

O come, let us adore Him!
O come, let us adore Him!
O come, let us adore Him– Christ, the Lord!
(Repeat)

Words, Latin Hymn; attr. to John F. Wade; Music attr. to John F. Wade

Angels, from the Realms of Glory

Angels, from the realms of glory,
Wing your flight o'er all the earth.
Ye who sang creation's story,
Now proclaim Messiah's birth.

Come and worship. Come and worship.
Worship Christ, the newborn King.
Worship Christ, the newborn King.
Worship Christ, the newborn King.

Words by James Montgomery; Music by Henry T. Smart

I Love You, Lord Jesus

I love You, Lord Jesus,
I love You, Lord Jesus;
You came to this earth for me.
I love You, Lord Jesus,
I love You, Lord Jesus;
You came to this earth for me.

Words and Music by Marty Parks